MW00760043

A Gift For My Friend:

FROM:

_____

OCCASION:

_____

DATE:

_____

A friend loves at all times.

PROVERBS 17:17

Smiles

for My Friend

MARK GILROY
COMMUNICATIONS

Smiles for My Friend™

Published by Mark Gilroy Communications, Inc.,
6528 E. 101st Street, Suite 416, Tulsa, Oklahoma 74133-6754
www.markgilroy.com

Copyright © 2004 By Mark Gilroy Communications, Inc., Tulsa, Oklahoma

Design By Jacksondesignco, llc, Siloam Springs, Arkansas

Illustrated by Abbi J. Brown, England, Copyright © 2004

Written by Christy Phillipe with Mark Gilroy and Jessica Inman

ISBN 0-9721682-4-9

Printed in Hong Kong

A Smile for My Friend

Smiles is a cup of cool water on a hot day. . .a phone call when you are lonely. . .a bouquet of roses on your birthday. . .a hot bath after a tough day at work. . .a kind word in the midst of a busy and impersonal world.

Let the charming stories, inspiring quotes and Bible verses, and the positive affirmations of Smiles bring cheer to you and your treasured friends. So sit back, relax, and enjoy as you are reminded of the wonderful ways God has blessed you and the countless reasons you can walk though life with faith and optimism, and of course, a smile on your face!

An anxious heart weighs a man down,
but a kind word cheers him up.

PROVERBS 12:25

Freckles and Wrinkles

True friendship is seen through the heart,
not through the eyes.

ANONYMOUS

An old woman and a little girl whose face was sprinkled with bright red freckles spent the day at the zoo. The little girl joined a group of children who were waiting in line to get their cheeks painted by a local artist.

"You've got so many freckles, there's no place to paint!" a boy in the line cried.

Embarrassed, the little girl dropped her head. The old woman knelt down beside her. "I love your freckles," she whispered.

"Not me!" the girl replied.

"When I was a little girl I always wanted freckles," the woman said, tracing a finger across the child's cheek. "Freckles are beautiful!"

The girl looked up. "Really?"

"Of course," said the woman. "Just name one thing that's prettier than freckles."

The little girl peered into the old woman's smiling face. "Wrinkles," she answered softly.

Friends see the true beauty that is within the other.

The Language of Laughter

Shared laughter is love made audible.

IZZY GESELL

Crystal was a five year old who loved everyone who crossed her path. When she was introduced to an Amish girl her age, within minutes they scampered off hand-in-hand to play. Sylvia, the Amish girl, spoke with a charming but unique and rare Pennsylvania Dutch dialect. Both moms watched cautiously, but despite the language barrier, Crystal and Sylvia got along marvelously.

That night Crystal's mother asked her, "Could you understand all the things Sylvia said to you?"

"No, not everything," Crystal replied.

"But you played together so nicely. How?" her mommy asked.

"Oh, that's easy. We understood each other's giggles."

True friends understand the language of shared laughter.

Hi, Lady!

*Getting people to like you is only
the other side of liking them.*

NORMAN VINCENT PEALE

$\mathcal{F}$riendship takes a little work in our neighborhoods filled with privacy fences, garage door openers, and other relationship barriers.

One morning as Lynn walked down the driveway to her mailbox, she noticed her neighbor, someone she had lived across the street from for over a year but never spoken to, walking up his drive.

To her surprise he called out cheerfully, "Hi, lady!"

Wanting to be friendly, Lynn waved back to him and exuberantly exclaimed, "Hi, buddy!" as a greeting in return. Looking startled, the man quickly disappeared into his house.

As a puzzled Lynn carried the mail up the drive to her own house, her teenage daughter sardonically explained the man's surprise. He was greeting their next-door neighbor's dog—who was named "Lady"!

Sometimes friendship takes a little work—
and the willingness to make the first move.

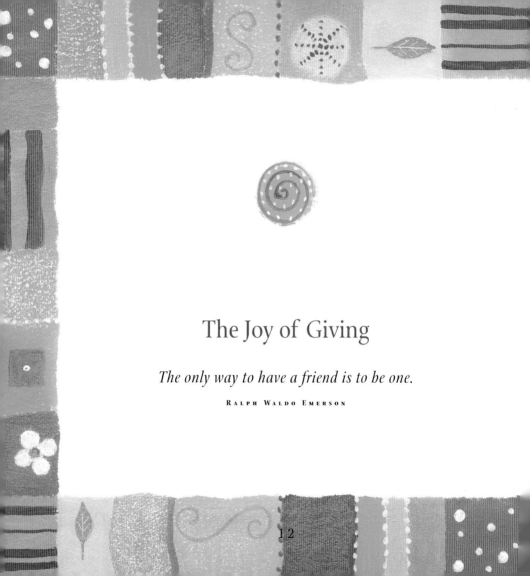

The Joy of Giving

The only way to have a friend is to be one.

RALPH WALDO EMERSON

As a Christmas present, Michael received a brand new car from a close friend who had just inherited a large sum of money.

Several weeks after the holidays, as Michael left the office to go home, a shabbily dressed man stood near his parking spot, admiring his new wheels. "Hey man, is this your car?" the man asked.

Michael nodded with a gulp. "My friend gave it to me for Christmas."

The man was astonished. "You mean, your friend gave it to you, and it cost you nothing? Man, I wish ..."

Michael anticipated what the wish would be—that the man, too, would love to have such a generous friend.

"I wish," the man continued to Michael's amazement, "that I could be a friend like that."

In friendship, giving is just as wonderful as receiving.

The Fragrance of Friendship

*If I had a single flower for every time I think
about you, I could walk forever in my garden.*

CLAUDIA GRANDI

$\mathcal{M}$ary is one of my best—and most unique—friends. She loves collecting and wearing a breathtaking—literally—array of perfumes. Many of her friends and relatives, familiar with Mary's predilection for fragrances, love to buy her new fragrances as gifts.

Mary is also a cheerful and loving person who enjoys hugging other people—friend or stranger! When Mary gives me a hug, her fragrance rubs off on me, and I remember her warmth and friendship for hours because the scent of her perfume lingers on my clothing.

When I think of Mary, I think of her cheerfulness and the sweet-smelling friendship she brings. I hope that my friendship, too, "rubs off" on others and is a fragrance that brings a smile to their face when they think of me.

The glow of warmth and affection remains
long after friends part company.

A Half Dollar Bill

God loves a cheerful giver.

2 CORINTHIANS 9:7

$\mathcal{T}$he young family of five filled up half a pew each Sunday morning during worship service at their church. One of their rituals was for the father to give each of his children a crisp, new dollar bill to put in the collection plate when the offering was taken.

One Sunday, their five-year-old son, Joey, brought his best friend, Thad, to church. The father had not put enough singles in his wallet to give a bill to Thad, and was hoping the young boy wouldn't notice.

As the offering plate was passed toward the family, the father looked down the row to his left. To his surprise and joy, he saw Joey, without a second thought, tear his crisp dollar bill in half and then hand a "half dollar" to Thad to place in the plate.

Sharing is a true hallmark of friendship.

A Comfortable Silence

*True friendship comes when silence
between two people is comfortable.*

DAVE TYSON GENTRY

18

$\mathcal{M}$aude was an elderly, despondent woman, living out her final years in a nursing home. She refused to speak to anyone or request anything. To the casual eye, she was merely staying alive. Her only activity each day was to rock back and forth in her creaky old rocking chair.

The old woman didn't have many visitors, but one young nurse, on the mornings she worked, would go into Maude's room, pull up another rocking chair next to her, and quietly rock with her.

To the young nurse's astonishment, after months of silence, Maude finally spoke.

"Thank you," she said. "Thank you for rocking with me."

Friends don't always need words—sometimes they simply need to sit and rock next to each other.

The Sighs of the Heart

*The best and most beautiful things in the world cannot be
seen or even touched. They must be felt with the heart.*

HELEN KELLER

She keeps repeating it over and over again!" Stacy's mom said in exasperation. "We've been back to this shelter at least five times."

"What is she saying?" asked the volunteer at the pet adoption agency.

"'Puppy size!' I don't know what she wants, but I wish she'd make up her mind. We've looked at big and tiny dogs, but it doesn't seem to make a difference. She won't decide."

Suddenly, they heard a squeal. "I've found him!" Stacy cried out.

"Thank goodness! What made you know it was the right one?"

"Don't you remember, Mommy? You told me, 'Love depends on the sighs of your heart.' I knew I would find the right puppy if it sighed when I held it in my arms."

Sure enough, the puppy snuggled up to Stacy and she smiled. "Mom, he loves me. I felt the sighs of his heart."

Friends hear both the words and the
unspoken yearnings of one another's hearts.

I Was Her Arms

When a friend is in trouble, don't annoy him
by asking if there is anything you can do.
Think up something appropriate and do it.

EDGAR WATSON HOWE

$\mathcal{B}$ob Butler lost his legs in a landmine explosion in Vietnam. He returned home a war hero, and 20 years later, he was a hero once again.

Hearing a piercing scream from the house next door, Bob pushed his wheelchair toward the neighbor's yard. When the dense shrubbery made pushing a wheelchair impossible, he got out and crawled. When he saw a three-year-old girl at the bottom of the pool, he dove in, pulled her to safety, and performed CPR until paramedics arrived.

When asked where his source of courage came from, he replied, "In the pool, I was her arms to swim; and then I was her lungs to breathe. Sometimes we need others to stand, or swim, or breathe for us. I've been blessed to have those kinds of friends in my life—it was my turn to be that kind of friend to someone else."

Friends dive into the pool and help each other in times of need.

Just Come Near

A friend is someone you can do nothing with, and enjoy it.

THE OPTIMIST MAGAZINE

While Stuart was serving as a missionary in Paraguay, a Maka Indian named Rafael came to sit on his porch. Stuart was eating and went out to see what he wanted. Rafael responded, "Ham, henek met."

Again Stuart asked what he could do for the man, but the answer was the same. Stuart understood what the man was saying, but its significance was new to him. "Ham, henek met" literally meant: "I don't want anything; I have just come near."

Stuart later shared the incident with a local veteran missionary who explained that it was Rafael's way of honoring Stuart. Rafael truly didn't want anything; he found simple satisfaction and pleasure just being in Stuart's presence.

Friends enjoy being near one another.

One Lucky Lady

You are only what you are when no one is looking.

ANONYMOUS

It had been a year since Susan became legally blind due to a medical misdiagnosis. It had been difficult, but the time had come for her to get on with life. She'd practiced riding the bus with her best friend, Mark, at her side, but today was her first solo venture. Mark was in the Marines and was shipping out to the Middle East later that week.

When she reached her destination and began to exit the bus, the driver said to her, "I sure envy you. It must be wonderful to be so well taken care of."

Susan didn't understand until the driver explained, "As you were boarding, a handsome man in a military uniform stood across the street watching over you until you got on the bus safely. You are one lucky lady."

Friends care for each other even
when the kindness can't be seen.

Pray With Me

*Carry each other's burdens, and in this way
you will fulfill the law of Christ.*

GALATIANS 6:2

$\mathcal{H}$ans was despondent when his wife, Enid, passed away. Worried because he no longer would eat or take walks, Hans' friends visited him regularly, but he remained lonely and depressed. Experiencing the "dark night of the soul," Hans told his friends, "I am no longer able to pray to God. In fact, I am not certain I believe in God anymore."

After a moment of silence, one friend said, "Then we will believe for you. We will make your confession and pray for you."

So the four men met daily for prayer, asking God to restore the gift of faith to their dear friend.

Many months later, as the four gathered with Hans, he smiled and said, "It is no longer necessary for you to pray for me. Today, I would like you to pray with me." The dark night of the soul had passed. The men had carried Hans to Jesus on their prayers.

True friends carry us when we can't carry ourselves.

I Packed Your Parachute

Strangers are friends you haven't yet met.

ANONYMOUS

Charles Plumb was a U.S. Navy jet pilot in Vietnam. After 75 combat missions, his plane was shot down, and Plumb parachuted into enemy territory, becoming a POW. He survived his ordeal, however, and eventually returned home.

While eating in a restaurant one day, he was approached by a scruffy looking man who said, "You're Plumb! You flew jet fighters in Vietnam and were shot down!"

"How did you know that?" asked Plumb.

"I packed your parachute," the man replied. "I guess it worked!"

Plumb couldn't sleep that night, thinking about the unknown man who'd saved his life. From that day on, he determined to always notice—and say thank you—those who "pack his parachute" each day.

Friends are those who render the simple services that make life safe and sweet.

Moving Mountains—and a Barn

*What do we live for if it is not to
make life less difficult for each other?*

GEORGE ELIOT

$\mathcal{H}$erman Ostry's barn floor was under 29 inches of water when a small dam broke and a creek flooded on his property. He needed a miracle—and fast—to salvage his barn and be ready for winter.

The Bruno, Nebraska, farmer invited a few friends to an old fashioned barn-raising. He needed to move his entire 17,000-pound barn to a new foundation more than 143 feet away. His son, Mike, devised a lattice work of steel tubing. He nailed, bolted, and welded the lattice on the inside and the outside of the barn. Hundreds of handles were attached.

After one practice lift, 344 volunteers slowly walked the barn up a slight incline, each supporting less than 50 pounds. In just three minutes, the barn was on its new foundation. And Herman had his miracle.

With faith in God—and the love
of friends—we can move mountains!

Dancing on Potato Chips

If you have made another person on this earth smile,
your life has been worthwhile.

SR. MARY CHRISTELLE MACALUSO

*R*ecently I had one of those days. Everything went wrong—including my plans for dinner. I should have stopped by the market, but I was too frazzled. Surely there'd be something to eat at home.

Opting for soup, I had a can open and in the sauce pan before I realized we were out of milk. Plan B was leftover baked beans, but that idea was nixed when I saw that the container was growing a healthy crop of mold!

Angry, I grabbed a bag of potato chips and pulled hard on the plastic corners. The bag split open and the chips flew sky high!

My cry of anguish was heard in the living room. My roommate, who had just returned home, rushed in and did the most helpful thing she could think of—and that I needed. She jumped into the middle of the pile of chips and started dancing!

I let out a laugh and started dancing too.

Friends can help you dance the discouragements and inconveniences of life away!

Simple Wonders

What a grand thing, to be loved!
What a grander thing still, to love.

VICTOR HUGO

A group of students were asked to list what they thought were the current Seven Wonders of the World. Though there was some disagreement, the following got the most votes:

Egypt's Great Pyramids • the Taj Mahal • the Grand Canyon •
the Panama Canal • the Empire State Building • St. Peter's Basilica •
China's Great Wall

While gathering the votes, the teacher noted that one quiet student hadn't turned in her paper yet. She asked the girl if she was having trouble with her list.

The girl replied, "Yes, a little. I couldn't make up my mind because there were so many."

The teacher said, "Tell us what you have, and maybe we can help."

The girl hesitated, then read, "I think the Seven Wonders of the World are: 1. to see; 2. to taste; 3. to touch; 4. to hear; 5. to feel; 6. to laugh; and 7. to love."

Those things we overlook as simple or ordinary are actually truly wondrous.

The love of friendship is one of the greatest wonders of the world!

A True Victory

Sometimes our light goes out but is
blown into flame by another human being.
Each of us owes deepest thanks to those
who have rekindled this light.

ALBERT SCHWEITZER

$\mathcal{D}$uring the 1960 Olympics, defending gold medalist, Al Oerter. and teammate Rick Babka were expected to take the gold and silver medal in the discus throw. Although Babka was very ill the night before the competition, he was ahead of his teammate after the first four throws.

On the fifth and final attempt, Oerter stepped into the circle, spun around with all the force he could muster, and set the world record for the discus, capturing the gold medal.

What allowed him to snatch victory from defeat? Prior to his final throw, Babka pointed out a minute flaw in Oerter's technique. A tiny adjustment was all Oerter needed to succeed.

Babka's lavish act of friendship probably cost him the gold medal, but no one could call him a loser in life.

Friends help each other win,
no matter how great the personal cost.

A Listening Ear

There is no greater gift than a sympathetic ear.

FRANK TYGER

One afternoon after the death of her grandfather, Jenny huddled on her bed, sobbing. Her mother sat beside her and asked, "What's the matter, honey?"

"I miss Grandpa, and I miss talking to him about my problems!" the girl said.

"I know, dear," sympathized her mother. "I miss him, too. But can't you talk to me?"

Jenny shook her head vehemently.

"Why not?" her mother persisted.

"Because you're what we talked about!" sobbed Jenny.

As children we may not always confide in our parents, and as adults we may choose not to discuss our problems with most of the people in our lives. But all of us need a trusted friend who will listen when times are tough!

True friends listen when we need to talk—and cry.

Let's Do Lunch

*Life's truest happiness is found
in friendships we make along the way.*

ANONYMOUS

"Let's do lunch," Jean would ceremoniously say to Linda each day. And Linda would officiously accept. Both, frazzled by clamoring middle school students and a ton of paperwork, looked forward to this oasis of friendship in the midst of a busy day.

They ate countless midday meals together through the years. Over yogurt fruit plates or macaroni and bean soup in the cafeteria, they talked about their kids, movies, even growing up as lonely bookworm teenagers. Yet inevitably, conversation would return to students and classes.

Looking back, Linda suspected that they had learned as much about teaching and human dynamics at the lunch table as they had in the classroom during college. New ideas and theories were born. Solutions to all sorts of classroom problems were hashed out.

"So much work accomplished, with so much joy."

Work becomes joyful when we turn friends into colleagues, and colleagues into friends.

A Friend in Need

*Praise be to the God and Father of our Lord Jesus Christ,
the Father of compassion and the God of all comfort, who com-
forts us in all our troubles, so that we can comfort those in any
trouble with the comfort we ourselves have received from God.*

2 CORINTHIANS 1:3-4

*I*n her first days of retirement, Betty went into a period of depression. She lost her feelings of self-worth. She saw a counselor, but nothing seemed to lift her out of her deep, black pit of misery.

Then one dismal Sunday afternoon she happened to be looking at a copy of her church's membership roll, noting the names of women who had recently become widows. Haven't seen them at church lately, Betty told herself. Why don't you visit them? said a small voice from within.

Betty wrote their names and addresses on a card, put on her coat, and headed out. At the first house, she found a woman alone, confused, and in need of medical attention. Betty, no longer despondent, took charge of the situation. Her depression disappeared immediately.

Almost instantaneously she began to thrive again, knowing she had a purpose and was following God's plan for her life.

Being a friend to someone else in need will help us smile as we overcome our own troubles.

I Knew You'd Come

Could we see when and where we are to meet again,
we would be more tender when we bid our friends goodbye.

MARIE LOUISE DE LA RAMÉE

$\mathcal{A}$lthough James was older than Ben, they did everything together throughout their childhoods. Later in life, they each joined the Marines and fought side by side in Germany during WWII.

During a fierce battle, amid heavy gunfire, they were given the command to retreat. As he was running for his life, James noticed that Ben was missing. Risking everything, James ran back into the gunfire, calling out for Ben. Soon his platoon saw him hobbling back, carrying a limp body in his arms.

James's commanding officer upbraided him: "You took a foolish risk—and your friend was already dead!"

"No sir, you're wrong," James replied. "I got there just in time. Before he died, his last words were, 'I knew you'd come.'"

Friends stick with each other until the end.

Just a Little Kindness

A little kindness from person to person
is better than a vast love for all humankind.

RICHARD DEHMEL

$\mathcal{H}$er clothes were old, and her shoes were dirty and torn. Most of the kids teased her, but I proudly did not join in. But even though I held my ground on not being mean, I tended to avoid her so the other kids wouldn't tease me.

When the school year was over, I was out with my mother when I heard a voice call out my name. It was her; the girl everyone picked on; the girl whom I'd deliberately avoided.

I quickly mumbled hello and started to walk away. But she caught my eye and said, "I wanted to thank you for being so nice to me in school. Thank you for being my friend."

I was glad for the little kindness I had shown her, but ashamed that I hadn't truly been the kind of friend she needed.

As we became the best of friends from that day forward—a friendship that has followed into adulthood—I learned that even the smallest acts of kindness plant the seeds for great relationships.

Kindness is the mark of true friendship—
and brings a smile to everyone's face.

Majestic Redwoods

Two are better than one, for if they fall,
the one will lift up his fellow.

KING SOLOMON
ECCLESIASTES 49:10

The Sequoia trees of California tower as high as 300 feet above the ground. Strangely, these majestic giants have unusually shallow root systems. Rather than go deep, the roots reach out in all directions to capture the greatest amount of surface moisture.

Seldom will you see a redwood standing alone. The danger is that high winds will quickly uproot it. Redwoods grow in clusters. Their intertwining roots provide support for one another against the storms.

Just like those giant Sequoia trees, we, too, need a network of friends to "stand with us" in times of trouble.

True friends gladly support each other
when the storms of life rage.

Just Call

The golden rule of friendship is to listen to others
as you would have them listen to you.

DAVID AUGSBURGER

$\mathcal{D}$ad, why don't you call some of your friends?" Denise said to her seventy-five-year-old father who had recently come to live with her.

Denise's dad had seemed a little down and more than a little lonely lately, but he still kept ignoring his daughter's suggestion. Finally he admitted the reason to Denise: "I don't have anything to talk to them about."

Denise's father is like many people who feel they need a reason to keep in touch with old friends. But things changed one day, when one of his old friends called him. Denise could hear her father laughing boisterously in the other room before hanging up after close to an hour.

When Denise asked what they had talked about for so long, her dad thought for a moment and then replied with a chuckle: "Well, I guess we didn't talk about much at all! It was just good to hear his voice."

Good friends don't need a reason to call.

Didn't Even Know Her Name

That best portion of a good man's life—his little,
nameless acts of kindness and of love.

WILLIAM WORDSWORTH

It could have happened anywhere, but this happened in New York City—a brief moment on a brisk day when Janie said goodbye to a friend.

Her friend was returning to her home overseas and would not be back. They met in their favorite park where every morning they'd walked our dogs—Janie with her bird dog, and her friend with a miniature poodle. Their animals sniffed each other as they talked.

"I'll miss you," the friend said.

"My mornings won't be the same without you," Janie replied. "You've made each day richer."

They stood for a moment, then Janie's friend and her poodle hurried away.

Janie did not know her friend's name, nor she Janie's, but for four years they'd been friends. They'd passed each other every day in a setting that was often cold, impersonal and unfriendly, offering each other the warmth of smiles and waves. And finally, after four years, they'd had their first conversation.

We won't be best friends with everyone—but we can be friendly to everyone.

Warm the world with friendliness and a smile.

What I Really Meant

Listening, not imitation, may be the sincerest form of flattery.

DR. JOYCE BROTHERS

$\mathcal{E}$nglish is a difficult language. Some signs posted in various establishments around the world for English-speaking guests betray just how difficult it can be to properly translate certain thoughts.

In a Copenhagen airline ticket office the sign reads: "We take your bags and send them in all directions."

A sign in a Paris hotel advised: "Please place your values at the front desk."

A Swiss menu proclaimed in English: "Our wines leave you nothing to hope for."

And the assurance in an Acapulco hotel stated: "The manager has personally passed all the water here."

It's so easy to miscommunicate—even when we speak the same language! The best way to truly understand is also the best way to make friends: Learn to listen well!

Friends pay attention closely and listen to both words and the heart until they understand.

Pulling Together

*No one is useless in this world who
lightens the burden of it for anyone else.*

CHARLES DICKENS

The man accidentally drove his car into a ditch out in the country. He was not hurt, but he was stuck and couldn't get his car out of the muddy channel. He walked several miles to the nearest farmhouse and asked the farmer for help.

The farmer said: "I have an old mule named Dusty. He can pull you out."

The farmer hooked Dusty up to the man's car, and when the ropes were in place, he snapped the reins and shouted: "Pull, Jack! Pull, Joe! Pull, Bill! Pull, Dusty!" Amazingly, the old mule pulled the car out of the ditch with ease.

The man was impressed, exceedingly grateful, and just a little confused. He asked the farmer: "Why did you call Dusty by four different names?"

The farmer replied: "Well, old Dusty's eyesight is just about gone. If he thought for a minute that he was the only one pulling, he wouldn't have tried at all!"

Loads are easier to pull—and life is much sweeter— when we have friends beside us to help.

Little Becomes Much

A single arrow is easily broken—but not ten in a bundle.

JAPANESE PROVERB

When Cheryl couldn't sell her home after moving to a new city, she decided to rent it out. Her tenants trashed the place and then skipped out before fulfilling their lease. She tried to sell the house again, but it sat on the market as she made monthly mortgage payments she couldn't afford. When foreclosure began to loom, Cheryl's friends stepped in to help.

They collected enough money to cover her next mortgage payment, buying her more time to sell the house at market value.

They found a realtor that was willing to help Cheryl perform necessary repairs to make her home more sellable.

And another friend—an attorney Cheryl could never afford—decided to take her case pro bono to ensure that Cheryl could stave off filing for bankruptcy.

Cheryl had been striking out, but when she shared her needs, her friends stepped up to the plate!

A little help from a number of friends
creates an enormous impact.

Hanging On Tight

There is no substitute for flesh-and-blood friends if we are to understand and learn to love ourselves.

TIMOTHY JONES

Shortly after Shelly's miscarriage, she met up with a friend whom she hadn't seen for several weeks. Janet suddenly pulled Shelly into her arms and whispered, "I'm so sorry about..."

She didn't finish the sentence, afraid to say the wrong thing. After a moment or two, Shelly released her hold, but Janet didn't. She just kept on hugging fiercely. Shelly squeezed back, but again finished before Janet did. Shelly hugged again, stopping only after Janet released her.

When Shelly stepped back, she realized on an emotional level that Janet had shown her more than love in that moment than she had felt the entire previous month. She'd shown her she'd hang on to her friend as long as her friend needed her.

Comfort comes through the love
of a friend who won't let go of us.

There All the Time

God doesn't always give us the friends we want;
instead He gives us the friends we need.

TIMOTHY SLEDGE

$\mathcal{A}$ngie desperately wanted to join a sorority in her freshman year of college. How much easier it would be to make friends, she reasoned. She participated in Rush Night and tried to conform to everything she thought the sorority would want. She was devastated when she learned that she hadn't made the cut.

The next day, Angie moped around, filled with insecurity. She kept going over the events of the previous day in her mind. What about me did they not like? But later that evening, two old friends from high school knocked on her door: "Hey, wanna grab a pizza?"

She hadn't thought of food all day and suddenly realized how hungry she was. As she threw on a jacket and grabbed her purse, Angie whispered a quiet prayer, *Lord, thank You for giving me true friends who were there all the time.*

Sometimes the friends we want
and need most are right in front of us.

The Personal Touch

I value the friend who for me finds time on his calendar, but I cherish the friend who for me does not consult his calendar.

ROBERT BRAULT

$\mathcal{J}$erry Rice, who played most of his football career for the San Francisco 49ers, is considered by many experts to be the best wide receiver to ever play in the NFL. A television interviewer once asked him, "Why did you attend a small, obscure university like Mississippi Valley State University in Itta Bena, Mississippi?"

Rice responded, "Out of all the big-time schools to recruit me, MVSU was the only school to come to my house and give me a personal visit." The other schools had sent cards, letters, and advertisements, but only one showed Rice personal attention.

How much more important is the personal touch of a friend in matters of the heart, soul, and spirit!

*Friends understand the importance
of the "personal touch"!*

In One Voice

*A friend hears the song in my heart
and sings it to me when my memory fails.*

ANONYMOUS

*I*t was one of those mornings when the church soloist didn't get up on the right side of the bed. Robert, an accomplished tenor, began his number that Sunday morning, but he soon began sweating profusely in embarrassment, as he missed cues and notes, his voice faltering as his confidence flagged.

Looking up from the music, ready to simply apologize to and quit before the sizable crowd, he saw that people in the congregation were pulling out hymnals to locate the words to the song he was attempting to sing.

One voice joined him so he kept singing. By the second verse, the entire congregation had joined Robert in a now triumphant anthem.

By the third verse, Robert was beginning to find his range. By the fourth verse, his tenor voice was soaring. On the fifth verse, the congregation fell absolutely silent, as the tenor sang the most beautiful solo of his life.

Friends help us sing the song of life.

Keep On Smiling

She is clothed with strength and dignity;
she can laugh at the days to come.

PROVERBS 31:25

$\mathcal{B}$ailey, our 5-year-old granddaughter, wiped the cleansing cream from around my eyes, part of our nighttime ritual before prayer and lights out.

Peering closely at my skin, she exclaimed, "Grandma Kitty, you have way too many wrinkles!" Only that morning I'd come to the same depressing conclusion. "You've got to stop smiling so much!" she added.

Always looking for potential learning lessons, I replied, "Grandma will never stop smiling."

"Why?"

"How do you feel when someone smiles at you?"

"I think they like me."

"That's why I'll never stop smiling."

"Okay, Grandma, you can smile all you want to."

What was meant to be a learning lesson for Bailey taught me something I needed to remember.

Our lack of wrinkles will never spread joy, but our smiles will.

Thursday Afternoon Golf

Friendship is one of the sweetest joys of life.
Many might have failed beneath the bitterness
of their trial had they not found a friend.

CHARLES SPURGEON

Stan and Richard have played golf every Thursday afternoon for more than ten years. They are very different types of men, from their personalities to their professions. Stan, loud and outgoing, owns a small TV repair business; Richard, quiet and introverted, is a commercial artist. But their afternoons on the course are an important ritual that neither violates if he is in town.

"We say that we do it for the exercise and fresh air," says Stan, "but we really want to check in with each other once a week. Make sure we're both doing okay. Provide a little accountability and encouragement."

Last year, Richard lost his job and was out of work for almost six months. "Without a doubt the Thursday afternoon talks with Stan," he said, "pulled me through until I got back up on my feet."

Time spent with friends helps us
to handle the pressures of life.

What's Your Name?

*We need old friends to help us grow old
and new friends to help us stay young.*

LETTY COTTIN POGREBIN

$\mathcal{B}$etty and June, two elderly women in the same neighborhood, were discussing the problems of growing older.

Betty commented with a dry wit, "The worst thing is when your memory starts to go. I've known you all my life and I can't think of your name. What is it?"

June thought for a moment and retorted back with equal energy, "Do you need an answer right now?!"

Friends grow with you through all of life's stages.

Not Letting Go

In prosperity, our friends know us;
in adversity, we know our friends.

JOHN CHURTON COLLINS

Anne and Debbie, two close friends and superb athletes, were mountain biking on a wilderness trail, when suddenly a 110-pound mountain lion sprang from the brush, pounced on Anne's back, caught the top of her head in his mouth, and began dragging her off the trail and into the brush.

Debbie screamed and grabbed Anne's legs, engaging in a desperate tug of war with the cat. Other cyclists who happened upon the scene began throwing rocks at the lion until it retreated and fled.

At the hospital that night, Debbie, through trembling lips, kept repeating, "I was not going to let go. . .I was not going to let go. . .I just told Anne, 'I'm never letting go!'" She later described the tenacity of the mountain lion: "The cat would not let go. He had such a hold on her. . ."

But the lion's tenacity was defeated by the faithfulness of a friend. Anne's life was saved by a friend who wouldn't let go.

Even in times of struggle and adversity, friends refuse to let go.

Just the Two of Us

*Life's truest happiness is found in
friendships we make along the way.*

ANONYMOUS

$\mathcal{M}$ichael Jordan is considered by many to be the greatest basketball player in the history of the sport. One night, he scored sixty-three points in a game. A Chicago Bulls teammate, who was neither a star nor a starter, was asked: "What's been the highlight of your NBA career?"

With his tongue planted firmly in his cheek, he answered: "It was the night Michael Jordan and I combined for sixty-five points."

Like playing basketball on a team with Michael Jordan, it may sometimes appear that we really aren't needed. But if we don't participate, it'd mean there wouldn't be anybody to pass Michael the ball—or score the final two points. Even Michael Jordan needs his teammates in order to win the game.

*Great friends make great teammates
in winning the game of life.*

Friendship and Off Days

*Laughter is not at all a bad beginning for a friendship,
and it is by far the best ending for one.*

OSCAR WILDE

$\mathcal{P}$am and Beth's hectic schedules made it nearly impossible to schedule a day in which the sisters could buy their mom a joint birthday gift, especially during the holidays. On their only day off, they finally met at the mall in the afternoon, with a small window to try to find the perfect gift. But everything that could go wrong—including the correct meeting place—did go wrong, and time slipped away all too quickly.

Frustrated and anxious, they pressed through the crowd. Then, at the same moment, a store advertisement caught their eyes. It read:

ONE DAY ONLY. . .EVERYTHING OFF!"

"That's for sure!" both exclaimed aloud, thinking how "off" their one day had been. Instantly, they burst into laughter and their spirits—and day—immediately improved. (And yes, their mother enjoyed her gift certificate that year.)

Laughter bonds friends—even when
everything goes wrong.

Uncomfortable Friendships

Don't make friends who are comfortable to be with.
Make friends who will force you to lever yourself up.

THOMAS J. WATSON

$\mathcal{G}$eneral William Westmoreland was once reviewing a platoon of paratroopers in Vietnam. As he went down the line, he asked each of them a question: "How do you like jumping, son?"

"Love it, sir!" was the first answer.

"How do you like jumping?" he asked the next.

"The greatest experience of my life, sir!" exclaimed the paratrooper.

"How do you like jumping?" he asked the third.

"I hate it, sir," he replied.

"Then why do you do it?" the General asked

"Because I want to be around guys who love to jump!"

Friends challenge each other to be better than they are.

Don't Lose Your Song

Show me your friends, and I will show you who you are.

THOMAS CARLYLE

Cheryl wanted a bird that would fill her home with song. She went to the pet shop and brought home a lovely yellow canary whose song was unusually beautiful.

During the summer, it seemed a shame to keep the bird pent up inside the house all the time. So Cheryl placed the canary's cage in a nearby tree for the bird to enjoy the sunshine and the fresh air. Many sparrows frequented the tree and were attracted to the cage. At first the canary was frightened, but soon he seemed to enjoy his companions as he sang away.

Then gradually and almost imperceptibly, he lost the sweetness of his song. By the end of summer, his singing was little more than the twitter of the sparrows. Spending time in the wrong environment caused Cheryl's canary to lose his finest song.

When someone robs us of our song, we, too, must make the painful choice of separation.

*Choose friends who will help you sing
the song God has put in your heart.*

Creating Something Beautiful

We are each of us angels with only one wing,
and we can fly only by embracing one another.

LUCIANO DE CRESCENZO

*H*ope and Courtney were best friends who shared an apartment together. Unfortunately, just before Christmas, Courtney was laid off from her job and Hope was forced to take a medical leave. Money was tight for both of them, and they wondered if they could afford a Christmas tree.

Late Christmas Eve, they happened to pass a lot where "leftover" trees were priced at $3.00 each. Suddenly Hope had an idea. They bought two trees, each with damaged branches on just one side.

Later, back in their apartment, after a flurry of activity, they gazed in wonder at their creation. They had trimmed the bad branches and then wired the two battered trees together to create a lush and beautiful Christmas tree.

It's like our friendship, thought Courtney. *When we have someone else to help our weaknesses, together we can create something truly beautiful.*

Together, friends create something of beauty.

Friends of Jesus

As the Father has loved me, so have I loved you. Now remain in my love.

JESUS
JOHN 15:9

$\mathcal{B}$efore Sharon tucked her daughter, Amy, into bed each night, they always read a Bible story together. Flipping through their children's Bible one night, Sharon pointed to an illustration of Jesus surrounded by His disciples. She asked Amy to explain the story in her own words.

Looking at it, Amy said, "Mommy, this is a story about Jesus. And here is a picture of Him and all his friends—Matthew, Mark, Luke, John, Acts, and Romans!"

Even if she wasn't quite right on the names, Amy understood how Jesus felt about the people who were close to Him in life.

Whatever your name—and whether others get it right—Jesus wants to be the Friend you most need in life!

Friendship with God is the greatest joy in life.

The Smell of New Clothes

It is one of the beautiful compensations of this life that no one can sincerely try to help another without also helping himself.

CHARLES DUDLEY WARNER

A missionary and his family visited in Sheila's home in the United States while raising funds. He had been serving in a warm climate and it was obvious that in the cold region where he and his family were headed next, their clothing would be inadequate. After the visit, Sheila decided to outfit the entire family with new clothes. She went shopping and sent the care package right away.

It didn't take long for a letter to come from the missionary, now a close family friend: "We cannot believe the gift you have sent. All of us had forgotten how wonderful the smell of new clothes is! God bless you, our dear friends!"

Sheila knew what he was talking about, for she, too, was inhaling a lovely aroma—the sweet, wholesome fragrance of being a "dear friend."

Friendship is a sweet-smelling fragrance in our lives.

All for One

*An arch consists of two weaknesses, which leaning
against one another make a strength.*

LEONARDO DA VINCI

$\mathcal{M}$y husband, a science teacher, once explained to me that when the roots of trees touch, there is a substance present that enables cooperation and reduces competition between them.

This unknown fungus creates a biological link between the roots of different trees—even those of dissimilar species. A whole forest may actually be linked together beneath the ground. Therefore, if one tree has access to water, another to nutrients, and a third to sunlight, all of the trees have the means to share with one another.

Just like trees in a forest, we need our friends to provide support and strengthen for one another.

Friends are linked to one another through sharing.

Open Doors

You can make more friends in a month
by being interested in them than in ten years
by trying to get them interested in you.

DALE CARNEGIE

I was always frustrated at how people would retreat into their shells after the Christmas holiday season was over. The trees would be piled high for trash. The lights got packed. The doors closed. Last year, I decided to give people a reason to come together.

I put up a sign that said, "Come for Coffee," with a date and a time when I thought most people would be available. I suggested they bring something to share.

I reserved the community area by the front entrance. I bought a 36-cup coffee maker and set it up 15 minutes before the time. I figured the worst thing that could happen was I would have a lot of coffee to drink alone!

But they showed up! Grandmothers with trays of cookies. Students. People coming home from work. I counted about 45 people. I couldn't believe it.

I rediscovered that when you open the door of hospitality, strangers become friends!

Open the door to new friendships in your life.

A Prayer for My Friend

Your love has given me great joy and encouragement.

PHILEMON 7

Dear God,

I am so grateful for the wonderful friend you have brought into my life to help me on my journey. I have been challenged and encouraged. I am so in awe that when I grow closer to You, I grow closer to my friends.

You alone are perfect and only You are absolutely trustworthy, but thank You that You have enriched my life with a friend who feels like a gift from You to me!